THE

I Ching

A GUIDE TO
YOUR DESTINY

Tui

(THE JOYOUS; PRONOUNCED DWAY)
IMAGE: WATER COLLECTED, AS IN A
MARSH OR LAKE
FAMILY RELATIONSHIP: YOUNGEST
DAUGHTER
ASSOCIATIONS: JOYFULNESS,
SATISFACTION, PLEASURE

Collected water suggests stillness, completion, and serenity. A feeling of joyousness pervades.

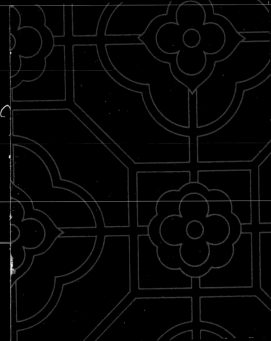

The
I Ching
A Guide to Your Destiny

Paul Lipari

ARIEL BOOKS

Andrews McMeel
Publishing
Kansas City

www.andrewsmcmeel.com

ISBN: 0-8362-5219-5
Library of Congress Catalog Card Number: 97-74522
Photos on pages 28–29 courtesy of Robert Egan

Contents

What Is the *I Ching*?   7

Seven Steps for Using the *I Ching*   15

    1. Formulating Your Question   19

    2. Tossing the Coins   24

    3. Structuring Your Lines   33

    4. Your Two Trigrams   36

    5. Interpreting Your Hexagram   43

    6. Reading the Changing Lines   46

    7. Your New Hexagram   52

The Eight Trigrams   61

If some years were added to my life, I would give fifty to the study of the *Yi* [I Ching] and might then escape falling into great errors.

—Confucius

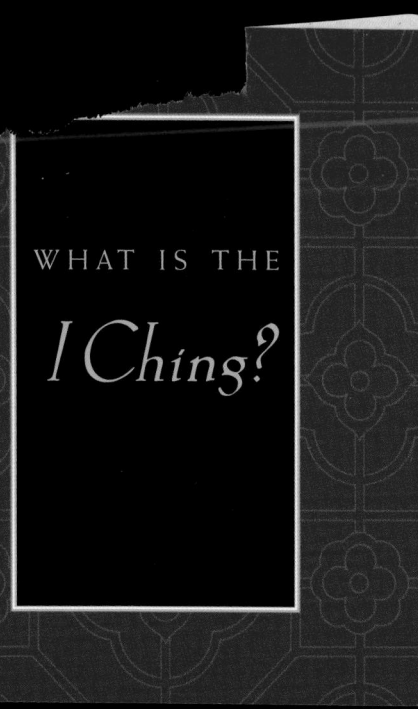

WHAT IS THE
I Ching?

The *I Ching*, or Book of Changes, is one of the great ancient classics of Chinese literature and philosophy, a work of wisdom and divination, process and change, that has held sway over the Chinese imagination for at least three thousand years, and possibly a good deal longer. It began as a collection of oracles used for fortune-telling, but centuries ago it achieved far greater richness and depth, and became nothing more or less than a reservoir of life's infinite possibilities; and you can use it today not merely for general understanding but to ask specific questions and obtain specific answers.

The core of the Book of Changes lies in sixty-four hexagrams, figures consisting of six broken and unbroken lines piled on top of one another into an elegant box. Each line within a hexagram symbolizes a different state of progress, process, and change; and every hexagram is an answer, or rather a network of answers, to any question you might want to ask. All of them together, according

此心此

to John Blofeld, who translated the *I Ching* into English over thirty years ago, "symbolize the entire sequence of changes through which everything in the universe, at all levels from the microcosmic to the macrocosmic, passes in continuous cycles." Difficult, mysterious, and enigmatic, the *I Ching* is a powerful tool for understanding the present, past, and future.

But the *I Ching* is not a book you merely read: You must *use* it. It is unlike any religious, philosophical, or psychological work in the Western tradition, because it does not instruct a passive reader as to what a "wise man" would do in certain situations or what the meaning of life is. Instead it will allow you, and even show you, how to puzzle out wisdom and life's meaning for yourself. It could well be considered the first interactive text in world history, because you have to work with the *I Ching* and talk to the *I Ching* in order for it to respond.

SEVEN STEPS

FOR USING

THE

I Ching

Seven basic steps are involved in consulting the Book of Changes. They may seem strange at first, but each will become clear as you work through the sections that follow.

1. Formulate your question.

2. Toss coins to determine what your lines will be.

3. Stack or structure the lines to build your hexagram.

4. Begin by interpreting the two trigrams that form the hexagram.

5. Read and interpret the hexagram as a whole.

6. Read and interpret the individual changing lines.

7. Read and interpret the second hexagram that those changing lines will form.

1

Formulating Your Question

The *I Ching* can answer anything, from *What should I wear to the prom?* to *Will I find happiness with the person I'm falling in love with?* The more specific your question, the more useful—and powerful—the answer will be. *What can I do to better myself* (morally, financially, etc.)? How can I stop smoking/drinking/overeating? Will I ever find the path to true wisdom? There are millions of possible questions.

Questions will never be answered with a simple yes or no, because the *I Ching* is a complex tool for exploring the workings of the universe and the way they will unfold. The more you engage it and the more you open yourself to its suggestions, the more you will gain. Suppose your question is the following:

For some time I have been involved in a very important personal project, to which I have dedicated all my energy and faith, but I'm not sure it is worth all the sacrifices I have made. Are my prospects favorable in the long run?

A sample reading and interpretation will explore this question.

2

Tossing the Coins

Traditionally the Chinese used yarrow sticks to determine the hexagram, but nowadays we generally toss three coins. Special Chinese coins are available, on which one side, *yang*, is blank and the other, *yin*, is carved with figures, but you

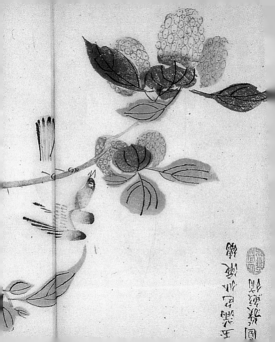

can just as easily use pennies, calling heads yang and tails yin.

Heads have a value of three; tails have a value of two. Toss all three coins at once. Four combinations are possible for each toss—HHH, TTT, TTH, and HHT— and the values are totaled up to determine what type of line you have obtained (see below). Toss the three coins six times in all, each toss yielding one line.

three heads = 9

This is considered an Old Yang line—a solid line in the process of becoming broken. That means it is changing into a yin line, and will be individually interpreted in step six of the sequence outlined above. It is represented thus:

three tails = 6

This is considered an Old Yin line—a broken line in the process of becoming solid. That means it is changing into a yang line, and will be individually interpreted in step six of the sequence outlined above. It is represented thus:

two tails + one head = 7

This is considered a Young Yang line, a solid line that doesn't move. It is represented thus:

———

two heads + one tail = 8

This is considered a Young Yin line, a broken line that doesn't move. It is represented thus:

— —

Our first tossing of the coins yields three heads, thus 9 and the line ―o― . The second toss yields a tail and two heads, thus 8 and the line ― ―→ . The third and fourth tosses repeat the first two: 9 and 8, ―o― and ― ―→ . The fifth gives us three tails, thus 6 and the line ―x― ; and the last, yet again, yields three heads, ―o― .

3

Structuring Your Lines

Hexagrams are built from the ground up.
Think of them as trees, whose roots provide the foundation, and which rise to
the sky. Your first line, ——o——, therefore
becomes the bottom line. Your second is
the line above, your third the line above

that, and so on, until the last line, —o—, fills out the top. You have constructed the following hexagram:

(9)	—o—
(6)	—x—
(8)	— —
(9)	—o—
(8)	— —
(9)	—o—

Four of these lines (three Old Yangs and one Old Yin) are changing lines and will be individually examined in a later step, but for purposes of building the first hexagram you need only remember that —x— is a broken line and —o— is a solid line. The hexagram you have built is hexagram 22, called Grace. (For interpretation of other hexagrams, a translation of the entire *I Ching* must be consulted.)

4

Your Two Trigrams

You should feel good about your project already, because a hexagram called Grace seems a promising start, but the first examination deals with your two trigrams. Like all hexagrams, Grace is composed of two trigrams, or three-line

figures, one on top of the other. The top one ☶ is *Kên* ("keeping still"); the bottom one ☲ is *Li* ("the clinging"). See the last chapter of this book for a detailed interpretation of all eight trigrams.

Kên is the force that stops things; this might be an answer or solution that will end the uncertainty you have faced thus far in your project or the many sacrifices you have made without any tangible return. *Kên* could be the signal that these difficulties are about to come to a halt. It also suggests stillness, strength, and immovable calm—desirable qualities to

Kên

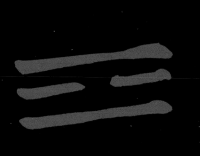

Li

bring to any risky and unsettled venture.

Li is light-giving, and represents the second daughter. This is an image of honor and fidelity—two qualities that have made your project superior, even if it has not received due recognition so far. The combination of this trigram with the first suggests that you should continue your present course no matter how old-fashioned it may seem. *Li* also stands for sun and fire, for the sudden illumination that banishes darkness; this clearly refers to the light you want to bring to this project that has taken so much from you, and which you now want to share with the world.

The two together create a curious combination of strength and clarity. This is a potent one-two punch; and no matter what your project may be—starting or reorganizing a business; writing a novel or an intricate computer program; moving to another country and starting completely anew; adopting a child; or anything else involving time, planning, sacrifice, and heart and soul—these qualities will act to stabilize your undertaking even as they provide the necessary sparks of energy.

5

Interpreting Your Hexagram

Grace is a very positive hexagram, pointing toward probable success for your project, although with a note of caution. The combination of firm (solid) and yielding (broken) lines indicates a good balance between strength and weakness.

A balanced, reasonable outcome is likely as long as you do not attempt too large an undertaking. Take a good look at the scope of your project: Does it feel manageable? Does it deal with something you are familiar with? Are you prepared to scale it down if necessary?

Prioritize your actions and responsibilities. Avoid trying to "remake the world." Having a well-defined goal and proceeding in a straightforward manner will bring satisfaction and success.

6

Reading the
Changing Lines

Only the changing lines (values of 9 and 6) require individual interpretation. Your hexagram has four changing lines: lines one, three, five, and six. Each of these will have a bearing on the answer to your question.

NINE IN THE FIRST LINE. Do not take the easy way out. If you are to succeed, it must be by personal effort. If you have been expecting a team of volunteers to do most of the work on your project, this is your signal to change course and learn to go it alone. Avoid borrowing from others' successes and don't expect that things will always go smoothly. Your own feet will carry you to your destination.

NINE IN THE THIRD LINE. Perseverance is the key. Even if you encounter obstacles at every turn—discouraging

words, unanswered letters and calls, naysayers, or prohibitive costs—do not lose heart. Your steadfastness and refusal to give up will eventually triumph. Good fortune is probable.

SIX IN THE FIFTH LINE. Minor matters have great significance. Although small by comparison to others, your resources will ultimately be measured by the value of your presentation. Your overall direction is strong, but success in the larger project depends on close attention to the finer points as well. Sincerity, integrity, and grace are crucial.

Your ability to identify and overcome difficulties will bring good results.

NINE IN THE SIXTH LINE. Simplify, simplify, simplify. When things begin to fall into place and your plans pick up speed, avoid the tendency to scatter and expand too quickly. Too many branches topple the tree. Clear your desk. All your efforts up to now have been praise-worthy and you are capable of success if you manage it carefully. Look ahead with clear eyes and do not falter.

7

Your New Hexagram

Any hexagram containing either Old
Yin —x— or Old Yang —o— lines
will metamorphose into a new hexagram, because those lines turn into their
opposites. Old Yin, remember, are broken lines becoming solid, and Old Yang

are solid lines becoming broken. Now that you have finished your initial interpretation, these lines complete their journey.

On the left is your main hexagram, Grace. On the right is the new hexagram formed by the changing lines (first, third, fifth, and sixth).

——— becomes — —

— — becomes ———

— — becomes — —

——— becomes — —

— — becomes — —

— — becomes — —

This yields hexagram 8, called Union. Grace, your main hexagram, dealt with the present and the short term; Union deals with more distant events—a long-term prognosis. The second hexagram does not need to be interpreted as closely as the first, and individual lines do not matter.

Union is a promising but demanding hexagram. It is an image of cooperation and holding things together. Most of the effort in your project is yours alone, but at times you will need to work with others. You must strive for consensus while maintaining your personal integrity.

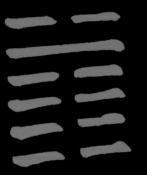

Union

Although patience and tolerance are valuable, if you wait too long to act, someone else may take the lead and things will go badly. On the other hand, a headlong rush to the finish will likely take you down an incorrect path. If you can balance the demands of cooperation and personal vision, you will meet with success.

Your project, no matter what it has or will cost you, is emphatically worth the effort.

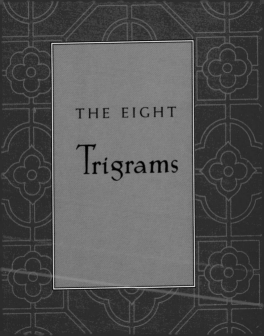

THE EIGHT

Trigrams

Each trigram has images and associations that have an important bearing on any reading of hexagrams.

Ch'ien
(THE CREATIVE; PRONOUNCED CHEE EN)
IMAGE: HEAVEN, SKY
FAMILY RELATIONSHIP: FATHER
ASSOCIATIONS: STRENGTH, STAMINA, POWER

This is the force of all creation, whether of things or feelings or ideas or natural forces. It is active and masculine, but without *K'un*, the receptive force, it can have no effect.

Ch'ien

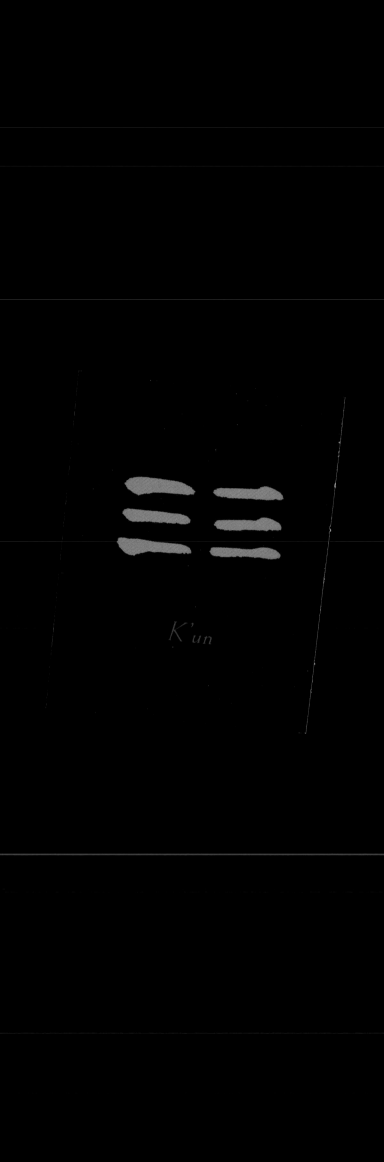

K'un

K'un

(THE RECEPTIVE; PRONOUNCED *KWEN*)
IMAGE: EARTH
FAMILY RELATIONSHIP: MOTHER
ASSOCIATIONS: RECEPTIVITY, CAPACITY,
MALLEABILITY, DEVOTION

As the Earth drinks water in order to make things grow, so *K'un* receives the power of *Ch'ien's* creativity. It is passive and feminine, but because true birth and development cannot take place without both *K'un* and *Ch'ien*, neither of them takes precedence.

Chên

(THE AROUSING; PRONOUNCED *JEN*)
IMAGE: THUNDER
FAMILY RELATIONSHIP: OLDEST SON
ASSOCIATIONS: MOVEMENT, ACTION

Whereas *Ch'ien* brings into being, *Chên* rouses into action. This is the irresistible force that brings energy, gives vitality, and calls forth the life essence.

Chên

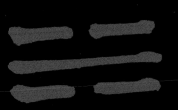

K'an

K'an

(THE ABYSMAL; PRONOUNCED *KUN*)
IMAGE: MOON; THE ABYSS; MOVING
WATER, AS IN RAIN, CLOUDS,
STREAMS, ETC.
FAMILY RELATIONSHIP: MIDDLE SON
ASSOCIATIONS: DIFFICULTY, PERIL

The abyss represents danger, as do
the destructive forces of floods, tidal
waves, and the like.

Kên

(KEEPING STILL; PRONOUNCED GEN)
IMAGE: MOUNTAIN
FAMILY RELATIONSHIP: YOUNGEST SON
ASSOCIATIONS: STILLNESS, RESTING, THE
QUELLING OF ACTION

Whereas *Chên* is the force that incites,
Kên is the force that brings motion to a
halt. Like the mountain, it is strong,
silent, and indomitable.

Kên

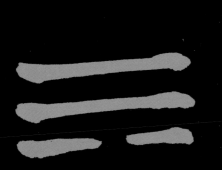

Sun

Sun

(THE GENTLE; PRONOUNCED SOON)
IMAGE: WIND; WOOD THAT GROWS, AS
IN BUSHES AND TREES
FAMILY RELATIONSHIP: OLDEST DAUGHTER
ASSOCIATIONS: OMNIPRESENCE, FLEXIBILITY

This is the gently penetrating and
pervasive force that is never seen but
whose effects are nevertheless felt. It can
be suspicion or a cooling breeze or the
attempts of a tree's roots to push up
toward the surface.

The Eight Trigrams · 73

L_i

(THE CLINGING; PRONOUNCED *LEE*)
IMAGE: SUN; FIRE; LIGHTNING
FAMILY RELATIONSHIP: MIDDLE DAUGHTER
ASSOCIATIONS: BRIGHTNESS, ELEGANCE,
RADIANCE; BEARER OF LIGHT

Li brings brightness, clarity, and interior illumination to what was previously dark. It represents reason and the process of gaining insight and understanding.

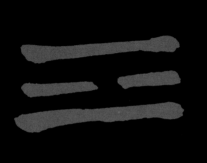

Li

Tui